Clear Skin, Healthy Skin

Clear Skin, Healthy Skin

BY ALAN E. NOURSE

Illustrated by Ric Estrada

FRANKLIN WATTS | **NEW YORK** | **LONDON** | **1976**

616.5
Nou

6834

Library of Congress Cataloging in Publication Data

Nourse, Alan Edward.
    Clear skin, healthy skin.

    (A Concise guide)
    Bibliography: p.
    Includes index.
    SUMMARY: A discussion of acne, its origins,
and treatments, with information on dandruff, body
odor, and suntans.
    1. Acne—Juvenile literature. 2. Skin—Care
and hygiene—Juvenile literature. [1. Acne. 2.
Skin—Care and hygiene] I. Title.
RL131.N68   616.5'3   76–12640
ISBN 0–531–00343–4

14460

Contents

Clear Skin,
Healthy Skin

An Adolescent Plague

You might call it an epidemic, except that it isn't catching, and it takes as many shapes and forms as the many young people it afflicts. No two people react exactly the same. A few of you—a very lucky few—may be completely untouched and sail through the dangerous years with only a few worried moments. But the rest of you will be hit sooner or later, one way or another, lightly or severely, no matter how you dodge or scramble. In some it strikes early and hard and hangs on for years. In others it may wait until age sixteen or seventeen or even twenty to occur. While still others suffer repeated flareups at totally unpredictable intervals. In a great many it will ultimately fade away like a bad memory (small comfort while it's there!). But even in these days of modern medicine far too many will be left with permanent scarring, often on the inside as well as the outside.

Historically it is one of the strangest and most universal afflictions known to man. (Only chicken pox strikes a higher percentage of potential victims.) Yet it can't be passed from person to person and it isn't really, strictly speaking, even a disease. It has never killed anyone yet, although victims sometimes say they wish they could die. Widespread as it is, hardly anybody talks about it in public, or in private either. Although you can't help getting it, you still feel oddly guilty when it appears. You search the back pages of magazines for news of miracle remedies, yet you have the strange feeling that nothing you find there will really work. (And you're right.) Above all, if you are in your teens or young adult years, *it's all yours.* Children below age ten are rarely affected, and if you can make it to age twenty or twenty-five, chances are it will quietly disappear. But the years in between can be murder.

When it turns up in full force it can make you do strange things. A Homecoming Princess will cancel her big date at the last minute and sit home miserable, convinced she is suddenly absolutely repulsive. A star quarterback will drop off the team because the chin strap of his helmet so seriously aggravates his condition. A girl previously free from the blight spends a week worrying about college entrance exams and comes up with such a spectacular case that she dreads showing her face on examination day.

A MATTER OF FACE

A case of *what?*

A case of acne, of course. The Teen-age Torment. Zits. Adolescent Pimples. Doctors call it *acne vulgaris.* (The *acne* comes from a Greek word meaning "face eruption"; the *vulgaris* means "commonplace," not "vulgar.") There aren't any *nice* names for it, and that tells you how it is viewed by society. We have fancy medical names for leprosy, trench mouth, or tapeworm disease, but acne is just acne, and nobody loves it.

Of course, one could argue that acne is a small price to pay considering the bounding, exuberant good health most of you enjoy in your adolescent years. The major children's diseases are behind you, and there are few if any serious "teen-age diseases." Your heart, lungs, and kidneys are generally in good shape. In fact, there is no *safer* time to be alive, from the standpoint of health, than the adolescent years. So why all the fuss about a few pimples?

It is largely a matter of face, and that is important indeed. Without any other complications, adolescence is already a tough enough time to live through. You are no longer children, yet you aren't quite adults either. The carefree childhood days are gone and everyone now expects you to answer for what you say, what you do, how you look, even what you think (especially when it doesn't agree with your parents). You are suddenly supposed to distinguish right from wrong, even when nobody else seems able to do so. Suddenly, your very bodies are changing on you, and you're supposed to act as if nothing is happening. Stand up to talk and your voice cracks. Try to make a dignified exit and you trip over your own feet. Work off your frustrations with physical exercise, and suddenly you're not nice to be near. And when you really try hard to present your best face to the world, what happens? You get acne.

The truth is that you have very little to cling to during these difficult years to keep up your confidence and good humor except your own *self-image* (the picture of yourself that you carry in your mind) and *self-esteem* (the way you feel about yourself inside). There is no other time in your life when your self-image and self-esteem are more important. If you really *like* yourself the way you see yourself, by and large, you're going to make it just fine. But when your self-image becomes flawed—actually, physically, undeniably flawed—then you can be in trouble. And when something turns up that you just can't help, which makes your image in the mirror somewhat less than lovely, you're going to hate it—you and all your friends who have the same thing happening.

THE LIES
PEOPLE TELL

Nobody needs to tell you just how hateful acne can be. And the world offers you little help in dealing with it. Your parents nag you unmercifully to "do something about it," though they don't say just what, or else they pretend it isn't there, which is maybe even worse. What's more, *people keep telling lies about it.* There is probably no other disorder surrounded by more ridiculous myths and false beliefs. Take the following, for example:

Acne can be prevented, so it's your own fault if you get it. Not true. Acne is the result of natural, normal, and inescapable changes that go on in your body beginning at puberty, and there is nothing you or anybody else can do to prevent it. Until these changes occur, there is nothing to prevent. Once they have occurred, the best you can do is to fight a condition that's already there. At least you're not alone: some 95 percent of *all* young people develop acne to some degree at one time or another, no matter what precautions they take. And with proper care you *can* reduce the severity of the condition when it appears and prevent the serious complications that can lead to permanent scarring and pitting of the skin.

Acne results from uncleanliness. This is another phony story. In fact, acne can and does develop in individuals who take the most careful pains with their personal hygiene. It is true, though, that those who have acne and fail to keep reasonably clean are likely to develop more severe and unsightly cases than necessary.

Acne is a giveaway that you have been indulging in sexual activities. This is a dreadful lie that causes more shame and embarrassment than any other. *There is no valid basis for this widely held belief.* True, acne does develop at a time of increasing sexual maturity. This is hardly surprising when you

realize that acne is actually *caused* by the action of some of the very same hormones that are responsible for normal sexual development. What is more, this is also a time when increasing sexual awareness quite naturally leads to sexual thoughts, sexual feelings, masturbation, and exploratory physical intimacy between the sexes. Such activities, however, neither cause acne nor aggravate it in any way. To blame a person for having acne on this account is both cruel and irrational.

Foods such as chocolate, nuts, candy, or cola drinks always aggravate acne and must be avoided at all costs. For many years even doctors told this to their unhappy adolescent patients, but many experts today say it's nonsense. We will have more to say about diet and acne in a later chapter. For now it is sufficient to say that *no* particular food need be completely avoided unless you yourself have discovered by trial and error that eating it causes *your* face to flare up.

Squeezing blackheads and pinching pimples will help reduce the amount of acne. In fact, precisely the contrary is true. Tempting as it may be to poke and probe, tormenting your face with fingernails or hairpins is the best imaginable way to spread infection and make your acne even more severe and difficult to treat than it already is. In "Home-Treatment Measures" we discuss alternative physical measures you can take that are safe and effective, and actually *will* reduce the severity of your acne.

Just quit worrying about it and after a while it will go away. Well, maybe—and then again, maybe not. You may have to wait a long time, and meanwhile untreated and uncontrolled acne can make a dismal and permanent mess of your face. The truth is that you don't *have* to just live with it, and in most cases you *shouldn't.* There are simple, effective, and sensible ways of dealing with acne today; to simply ignore it and wait for it to go away is nothing but foolish.

Most such stories about acne arise from plain ignorance and serve only to make the acne sufferers even more miserable than they already are, if possible. But there is no reason for such ignorance today. Acne arises in very specific ways for very specific, easily understood reasons. It has always been difficult to treat. It forever pops up again just when you think you've got it under control, but there *are* safe treatments that *do* help. In mild cases a simple "home remedy" approach using ordinary household materials or inexpensive over-the-counter medications may be all that is required. More severe cases may require a doctor's attention and certain prescription medicines for effective treatment. In either case, for the best results you will need some basic knowledge of what you are dealing with and a willingness to devote some time and attention to treatment. Few cases of acne are completely and permanently cured until the body finally adjusts to the hormone changes that bring it about in the first place; but when treatment is approached sensibly, virtually *every* case of acne can be significantly improved and most of the complications and distressing long-term aftereffects can be prevented. In short, the vast majority of acne sufferers can *control* the condition, if they go about it in the right way, until nature ultimately effects a cure.

The first step in sensible control is to know something about the normal structure and function of that remarkable organ system known as the skin, and then to see what changes come about to cause acne, and why.

The Origins
of Acne

It may seem odd, at first, to think of the skin as an organ system. When we speak of organs we normally think of such structures as the heart, the lungs, or the kidneys, which are all obviously vital to life. But the skin is also a vast and complex organ system, every bit as vital to life as any other. We could no more survive without skin than we could without brains or livers.

The skin, of course, is the face we present to the world, but it provides for more than mere appearance. First, it forms a tough protective covering for the entire body, keeping the moist inner tissues and organs from drying out. To do this job, it must grow and change as the body grows and changes from infancy to old age. Second, it must remain soft, elastic, and pliable, molding to the curves and angles of the body, allowing movement without overstretching or tearing. Equally important, the skin (together with the fatty layer that lies just beneath it) provides vital insulation for the internal structures, protecting them from excessive heat or cold. It also acts as the major heat control organ of the body, producing perspiration to cool the body's surface by evaporation when the interior becomes too hot, and providing a rich bed of capillary blood vessels to carry warm blood close to the surface when things outside get too cold. To remain soft and supple, the skin lubricates itself with a thin oily substance known as *sebum,* which is manufactured in special sebaceous glands. A fine growth of hair covers much of the skin except for the palms of the hands and the soles of the feet. This is more than just a throwback to times when our ancestors were more furry than we are; even today the hair on our heads protects us from heat loss from the head and neck when we are exposed to cold weather.

Finally, the skin has an important role keeping us informed about the state of things outside us by means of a vast network of delicate nerve endings. Some of these nerves are sensitive to heat or cold; others respond to being pinched, cut, or burned. Still others are sensitive to touch or pressure. The amazing thing is that all these capacities of the skin are packed into a layer of tissue that is no more than a quarter of an inch thick anywhere in the body and as little as one-sixteenth of an inch thick in sensitive areas such as the eyelids or the inner surface of the forearm.

THE STRUCTURES OF THE SKIN

To understand how acne arises, however, we must look more closely at the microscopic structure of the skin, for it is here the problem begins. This is a diagram of a small block of normal facial skin, drawn in three dimensions so that all the typical structures can be seen in their proper locations. The outermost layer has the simplest structure. Called the *epidermis* (from Greek words meaning "on or over the skin"), this layer consists of several thicknesses of dry, flat, surface cells fitted together like octagonal bathroom floor tiles. Since they are

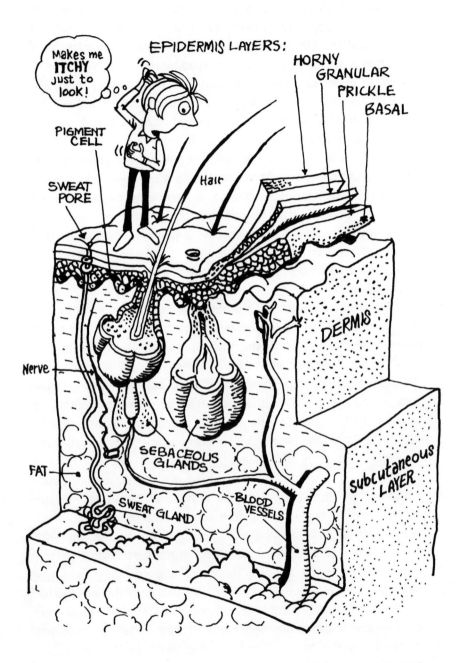

continuously exposed to drying, rubbing, or other damage, these cells are constantly dying and flaking off. In the course of a single hot shower you may scrub away a whole layer of these dead surface cells, which are replaced by the cells immediately below. In areas of heavy wear (such as the soles of the feet), multiple layers of these cells build up to form a protective pad or *callus,* but on the face this so-called horny layer of cells is only one or two cells deep.

Beneath the horny layer, cells of the epidermis are larger, rounder, and healthier. At the bottom is a so-called basal layer of cells filled with granules of a brownish black pigment known as *melanin.* It is the amount of melanin in these cells that gives the skin its natural color, whether it be the pinkish white seen in the Caucasian race (very little pigment), or the dark brown to intense blue black of the Negroid races (very heavy pigment).

The tough epidermis protects the thicker and softer underlayers of the skin—the *dermis,* lying just beneath the basal layer, and the fatty, elastic *subcutaneous* or "beneath the skin" tissue that lies still deeper. These layers have several distinctive structures. There are blood vessels—tiny arteries and veins—in the subcutaneous that send narrow capillary vessels up into the dermis to carry oxygen and nutrients to all the cells of the skin and to carry away waste materials. Tiny nerve endings also rise up through the dermis. But the most striking structure in the dermis is the *hair follicle* from which a hair grows up through a hollow sheath to emerge above the outer layers of the skin. Each hair follicle is equipped with an oil or *sebaceous gland* that secretes an oily material called *sebum* to help keep the skin's surface soft. On the face there are as many as one thousand sebaceous glands per square inch; yet in other regions (the palms of the hands, for instance) they are completely absent. In general, sebaceous glands are found wherever there is hair. They secrete the most oil on the scalp, the face, the back of the neck, the shoulders, and the chest.

In addition, the dermis and the lower subcutaneous tissues contain *sweat glands* that manufacture perspiration and carry it to the surface through narrow spiraling ducts. Although these glands are present all over the body, they are especially prominent in the armpits and groin, where they become very large and active at the time of puberty. In these sheltered areas the sweat becomes mixed with bacteria and surface dirt to create a characteristic body odor, which was perhaps useful to our remote prehuman ancestors for purposes of identification or mating, but is now generally considered offensive.

Finally, the bulk of the dermis is made up of a fibrous protein material known as *collagen* and many fibers of *elastic tissue* that, together, support the other structures of the dermis and give the skin its elasticity and its shape. Still deeper, the subcutaneous tissue contains a tougher network of fibrous tissue and fat that forms the soft "foundation pad" under the skin.

This, then, is the normal, healthy skin—obviously a vital, living organ system. Like the cells in any other organ system, those in the skin require oxygen and food materials; they carry on internal chemical reactions guided by enzyme systems; their health is supported by vitamins; and their activities are influenced by hormones.

THE DEVELOPMENT
OF ACNE

As the body changes and grows, so also do the structures of the skin. And it is during a major period of growth and change —the period from the beginning of puberty throughout adolescence into young adulthood—that acne arises.

Most of the changes during this interval involve both *body growth* and *sexual maturation.* Beginning sometime between the ages of ten and thirteen a number of powerful hormones are secreted in large quantities in the young person's body. Among these are the so-called sex hormones—*estrogens,* which are produced in the girls' ovaries and predominate as the female sex hormones, and *androgens,* which are secreted by the boys' testicles as the major male sex hormones. It is these hormones that are largely responsible for the development of mature sex organs in both male and female. They are also responsible for the familiar secondary sex characteristics that appear at the time of puberty, such as the growth and development of the female breasts and the enlargement of the voicebox and the deepening of the voice in the male. Oddly enough, both kinds of sex hormones are present in each of the sexes. They merely work together in different proportions to bring about either male or female sexual changes. In addition, these hormones produce a sudden spurt in physical stature and the development of mature musculature, more marked in the male in most cases, but present in the female as well.

Just as these hormones stimulate growth and development in other parts of the body, they also cause changes in the skin, particularly of the face, the neck, the back, and the chest. First, there is a marked enlargement of the sebaceous glands and a sharp increase in the amount of oily sebum that these glands produce. At the same time, the pores through which the sebum is discharged to the skin surface begin to enlarge. The skin—most notably around the nose, on the forehead, and on the chin—becomes coarser in appearance and noticeably more oily. Concurrently, certain of the sex hormones, primarily the androgens, bring about a change in the consistency of the sebum that is formed. Due to this hormone activity the sebum becomes thicker and more sticky in consistency, then almost waxlike. Instead of flowing freely to the skin surface it tends to jam up into waxy plugs in many of the pores. Once in contact with air and light, these plugs of sebum undergo chemical changes that turn them dark in color so that they become visible at the pore outlets as typical "blackheads" or *comedones* (the singular is *comedo*).

There is really nothing at all singular about the formation of comedones in the skin at this time of life. There is no way to stop them from forming and virtually everyone develops them. Their dark color arises from natural chemical changes and not from dirt, as so many people erroneously believe. For the most part, these waxy plugs are cleared away from the pores a bit at a time by simple gentle washing of the face with soap and warm water.

A few, however, are not cleared away—and it is here that the trouble begins. Further sebum production continues in these plugged-up sebaceous glands, causing the gland and the oil duct beneath the comedo to become distended, so that a raised bump appears. Then bacteria that live in the oil glands and ducts begin to grow in the backed-up sebum. At a certain point the overstretched walls of the duct break down, releasing the infected sebum into the surrounding tissue. This

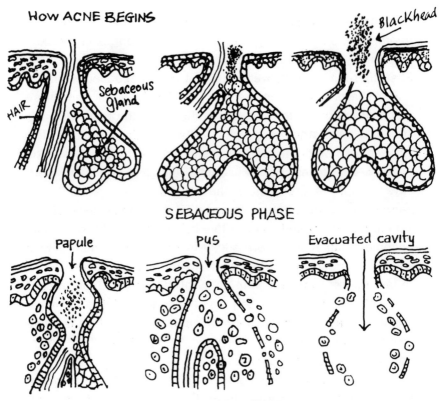

HOW ACNE BEGINS

Blackhead

HAIR

Sebaceous gland

SEBACEOUS PHASE

papule

Pus

Evacuated cavity

INFLAMMATORY PHASE

"invasion" of surrounding tissue by a foreign material causes an intense inflammatory reaction. The surrounding area becomes distended with fluid poured out by cells that have been irritated by the presence of the sebum. Nearby capillary blood vessels enlarge, bringing in an army of white blood cells to fight the invading bacteria. Very quickly the blackhead area is transformed into a typical raised, reddened pimple, known as a *papule*. As white blood cells and surrounding tissue cells are destroyed by the bacteria, the pimple is transformed into a small pus-filled pocket, or *pustule,* under the skin. In most cases the pustule will gradually work its way toward the skin surface where it can be seen as a "whitehead" and then, presently, will break to the surface, either naturally or due to external interference (picking with the fingers, for example, or too-vigorous washing with a rough washcloth). Once the pustule has broken, spilling its infected contents onto the skin surface, it will form a crust or scab and then, if the infection is not too widespread, it will heal with only a tiny scar that ultimately disappears, leaving no sign of its presence other than a slight roughening of the skin.

In the vast majority of cases, acne progresses this far and no farther. It involves the formation of a succession of pimples beneath the comedones that fester and ultimately open, drain, and then heal. But sometimes a more serious sequence of events occurs. Sometimes the infected papules become larger than usual, forming a deep-seated, tender, swollen lump in the skin. Often in such cases the pustular material does not escape to the surface, but forms a cavity or *cyst* beneath the skin, destroying the entire hair follicle and sebaceous gland in the process. Sometimes these cysts also work their way to the surface and drain. The ultimate healing, however, often leaves a reddish purple scar that gradually shrinks and permanently twists the overlying skin. Sad to say, many cases of the comparatively simple form of acne are actually converted to this destructive, cystic form when the acne victim digs and gouges at the skin in an effort to squeeze out comedones or break pustules. All too often such proce-

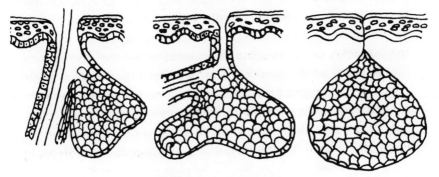

CYST FORMATION

dures do nothing but damage healthy cells around the papule and spread the localized infection into a larger and deeper area. In addition, such picking and poking may also spread infected material on the surface of the skin and introduce offending bacteria into more pores in the vicinity, so that still more pimples form. Finally, failure to keep the surface of the skin clean and free of oil promotes the further growth of bacteria. Efforts to conceal acne blemishes with oily or greasy makeup preparations on an already-too-oily skin trap bacteria and dead epidermal cells at the surface and lead to more pimples.

THE NEED
FOR TREATMENT

Obviously there is no single cause of acne. Hormone activity that enlarges the sebaceous glands and stimulates the production of oil is partly to blame. Chemical changes transforming the oily sebum into waxy plugs in the pores are partly to blame. Bacteria in the sebaceous glands and ducts are partly to blame. Picking and poking at the skin may convert a mild case of acne into a severe case, and the use of oily or greasy makeup for concealment may also play a part. As we might expect, acne appears most frequently in the places where the sebaceous glands become the largest and most active: around the nose, on the forehead, or on the chin. Less frequently it can appear on the back of the neck, the upper back, or the chest, and in a few cases, in the groin, on the legs, on the buttocks, or in the armpits. In most cases the disturbance first appears at the beginning of puberty, proceeds for a few years, and then gradually subsides. In some cases, however, trouble may not appear until the late teen years or early twenties. In general, outbreaks of acne tend to be more severe in the winter than in the summer, and girls often note a worsening of the condition just before a menstrual period—a reflection of the close relationship between acne and the shifting hormone balances within the body. Finally, it is possible that a person may inherit a family tendency to develop acne. Certainly it is true that one person may escape with only a few minor acne lesions, while others can be tormented with continuous severe acne that can lead to permanent scarring if it is not vigorously and constantly treated.

Fortunately there is no longer any need for anyone to suffer such permanent ill effects. Today even the worst case of acne can be effectively treated and immensely improved, while milder cases can be cleared up completely. In many cases treatment can be safely and effectively accomplished at home with the use of simple and ordinary medicine-shelf remedies. But when a case of acne fails to respond adequately to such home treatment, a doctor's advice should be sought and more potent medications, available only by doctor's prescription, should be employed. Even when a doctor must be consulted, however, treatment of acne need not be terribly expensive. The doctor's role is simply to evaluate which medicines and treatments may help the most in a given case and then to follow the patient's progress to be sure that all is going well. Above all, the success of any treatment program must depend upon the patient. The patient contributes the most, carrying out a treatment program faithfully and fully, perhaps over a long period of time.

In the next chapter we will first consider the logical measures that must be taken to bring any case of acne under control, based upon what we know of the origin of the condition. Next we will outline a simple, basic home-treatment program that can be used to keep acne under control in a great majority of cases. Later, we will consider additional measures that a doctor may take in dealing with severe, persisting, or complicated cases of acne.

Home-Treatment Measures

Obviously the time to start doing something about acne is when it first appears—long before deep-seated infection, cysts, and scarring have had a chance to develop. By taking effective measures early and continuing them as long as the condition is present, most young people can maintain relatively clear, healthy skin without doctors or costly remedies. But what treatment is most effective at this early stage? Since *any* treatment should logically be aimed at removing the *causes* of acne, whenever possible, we must consider these causes, one by one, and see what can be done to alter them.

THE GOALS OF TREATMENT

As we have seen, the major causes of acne are as follows:

1. Enlargement of the sebaceous glands and an increase in the production of oily sebum as a result of hormonal activity.

2. Transformation of the sebum into a waxy substance that plugs the pores to form blackheads or comedones.

3. Growth of bacteria in the plugged-up sebaceous glands, leading to infected papules or pimples.

4. Spread of the infection to surrounding tissue, with the formation of pustules that either drain to the surface or invade deeper tissues to form cysts.

Which of these causes might logically be alleviated by a simple program of home treatment? The activity of the sebaceous glands occurs under the influence of hormones, as part of a body-wide process of growth and maturation. Obviously there is no simple way to control this. Neither is there any way to prevent the sebum from hardening into waxy plugs that obstruct the pores, nor can we treat bacterial infection beneath the skin surface without the use of internal antibiotics, which would certainly not be a part of the simple home-treatment program.

Certain things, however, *can* be done to help keep the skin clear of comedones and free of surface bacteria. First, you can keep your skin free of excessive oil, dirt, bacteria, and debris by means of simple cleansing. Second, you can remove any other oil sources that could contribute to the retention of comedones in the pores and the growth of bacteria on the skin surface. Finally, you can use simple measures to encourage the comedone plugs to soften and come out by themselves, while refraining from digging and poking at them, and to aid the natural drainage of the small pustules that come to the surface as whiteheads. In short, although you cannot tackle the problem *internally* without a doctor's attention, you can do a good deal *externally* to minimize the problem and encourage healing. In the majority of cases these measures are *all that need be done* to keep minor acne under control and prevent it from becoming severe.

D-DIRT!

THE ROLE OF
SKIN CLEANSING

There is a widespread conviction among acne sufferers that the skin of the face is perpetually dirty and must be scrubbed repeatedly, day in and day out. This idea is not only ridiculous but also dangerous. Facial skin is far too sensitive to withstand continuous scrubbing. Too vigorous or frequent attempts at cleansing can easily lead to a mechanical and chemical *dermatitis* (skin inflammation) that can be as bad or worse than the acne. The goal of sensible skin cleansing should be to keep the skin *reasonably* free of oil and debris; to maintain reasonable dryness; and to discourage surface bacterial growth.

Moderation is the key. Twice a day—once in the morning and once in the evening, no more—the face should be washed thoroughly but gently with warm water, soap, and a soft washcloth. Scrubbing and rubbing is not necessary, nor is any prolonged massaging of soap into the skin. Soaping the skin for perhaps half a minute, followed by thorough rinsing, should be sufficient. If the acne is also present on the neck, the chest, the back, or the shoulders, these areas should be cleansed in the same manner.

What about special soaps? Virtually any facial-quality soap is satisfactory. Do *not* use strong laundry detergents or any abrasive soap, and avoid a complexion brush, which can scour the skin too severely. A wide variety of special "acne soaps" is available in the drugstore and is promoted as especially helpful. These soaps are uniformly expensive and produce little better results than ordinary facial soap, but they will do no harm if used as directed above. Try them if you wish, but expect no miracles. Certain other soaps found in the supermarket (Dial, for example) or the drugstore (pHisoHex or Septisol) contain antibacterial agents designed to destroy surface bacteria on the skin. Even the experts cannot agree as to the value of such medicated soaps; certainly they are perfectly suitable for use *as long as they do not seem to burn or irritate your skin.* Unfortunately, certain individuals can become extrasensitive to the antibacterial medications in these soaps. If you notice any sign of persisting redness, soreness, or itching, stop using them at once and return to an unmedicated soap.

Simple soap and water cleansing for a matter of two or three minutes twice a day will keep your skin satisfactorily clean and free of excessive oil. *Resist any temptation to squeeze or dig out blackheads,* even if a few of them seem particularly large. Once you have started you will find it virtually impossible to stop until each one has received attention and your face is raw and sore. Rather than digging, follow a simple procedure to help the skin expel the blackheads in a natural way. Using a washcloth and comfortably hot (*not* scalding) water, make a compress and apply it to the face where the blackheads are. The cloth should be wet but not dripping. Hold the compress in place until it begins to cool, then rinse in hot water and re-apply. Continue this hot compress procedure for perhaps five minutes. Then dry the face *gently* and take the third step in your skin cleansing routine: the application of a drying agent.

Perhaps the easiest, cheapest, handiest, and most effective such agent is plain rubbing alcohol, applied with the fingers or a cotton swab and allowed to air dry. Alternatively, use any of the *lotion-type* drying agents available over the counter in the drugstore. (Avoid creams or ointments, as they will merely *replace* the oil that you have been seeking to remove.) Many of these products contain sulfur, zinc, or resorcinol—a close chemical cousin of phenol, a powerful disinfectant. Many of these prepared lotions are flesh-colored and help conceal minor blemishes when they are applied and worn during the day. A good drying preparation for nighttime use is calamine lotion, either with or without phenol. (If calamine with phenol is used, dilute the lotion by half with water before applying. Discontinue use if persisting skin irritation occurs.)

The purpose of any such drying agent or lotion is to tighten the skin slightly so that the comedones previously softened by the skin cleansing and hot compresses tend to work to the surface. By making this three-step program (soap and water cleansing, hot compresses, and application of a drying agent) a morning and evening ritual and *leaving the skin alone in between* you can expect to see a marked clearing of your complexion within a period of one to two weeks. Don't be discouraged if nothing seems to happen in the first few days. Don't worry if the program seems to be producing *more* papules during the course of the first week. All that is happening is that the papules that had already begun to form are surfacing more rapidly under this treatment than they might have if they had been left alone. For the most part, they will clear up within the first week. Thereafter far fewer will form, and those that do will be smaller and less angry in appearance. At the same time, this simple treatment program encourages pustules to break and drain, clears infectious debris from the skin, and aids in healing. To gain the greatest benefit from this basic program of skin care, however, you will want to consider certain additional factors. These include such matters as hair and scalp care, the use of makeup, and attention to diet.

THE ROLE OF HAIR AND SCALP CARE

There was a time not long ago when even skin specialists regarded the hair and scalp as a "fountain of oil" that contributed to excessive oiliness on the face and aggravated acne. Girls who wore bangs were blamed for contributing to their acne, especially on the forehead, and long hair styles for boys were roundly condemned.

Today most experts dispute the view that oil from the hair and scalp contributes much to the severity of acne. Certainly daily shampooing is not necessary and in fact may be damaging to people who have fine or naturally dry hair. On the other hand, the hair does accumulate oil, dirt, and odors over a period of days, and in the interest of common good grooming you will want to keep it clean and free of dandruff. In general, shampooing the hair twice a week is sufficient. If dandruff is present it can usually be controlled with one of the so-called dandruff remover shampoos available over the counter at the drugstore. If the dandruff is heavy or really persistent, a medicated shampoo containing selenium compounds or other dandruff controllers, available on a doctor's prescription, may be needed. (For more about controlling dandruff, see the last chapter.)

If acne appears persistently under the hair overhanging the forehead and seems especially difficult to control, you might try styling your hair to leave your forehead exposed for an interval to see if the underlying acne clears up more readily. Boys with acne should shave whenever necessary to keep the upper lip, chin, and cheeks free of beard, since it is difficult to attain the desired dryness and relative absence of bacteria beneath a beard growth. If the beard is thick or fast growing, an electric razor may be best to prevent irritation and abrasion of the skin, but when the beard is light and slow growing, an occasional blade shave with a safety razor will do no harm.

WHAT ABOUT MAKEUP?

Obviously if you are seeking to control acne by keeping the skin cleansed, free of debris and oil, and reasonably dry, it does not make sense to apply powders, oils, pigments, perfumed chemicals, and other foreign materials to the same areas. Most modern makeup preparations have been carefully compounded by their manufacturers and will not harm healthy skin—but the common-sense rule for the acne sufferer is to use as little makeup as possible and to apply it only to those areas that are not afflicted with acne.

Fortunately a great many young women today prefer the "natural look," using little or no makeup at all, either for the face or for the lips. You may already have learned, to your grief, that even small amounts of lipstick can aggravate acne at the margins of the lips—perhaps the most unattractive place of all. Eye makeup, on the other hand, poses no threat. The use of upper lid tints, small amounts of mascara on the lashes, and a light application of shadow material on the lower lids—avoiding the cheeks—will have no effect on acne, since neither upper nor lower lids are affected by the eruption.

What about concealing makeup? Certainly it is tempting to try to hide angry red or violet purple blemishes with some kind of flesh-toned pancake makeup or liberal applications of a flesh-tinted lotion. Here you can only be guided by common sense: by far the best way to "cover up" acne blemishes is to treat and control them with the home-treatment program we have been discussing without adding foreign materials to your face. For a special date, party, or dance when you want to look absolutely your best, a small amount of concealing makeup carefully applied for a few hours can do no harm if you remove it when the event is over. But for everyday use, forget it. If you stick faithfully to your home-treatment program you will soon have far fewer blemishes that need to be concealed than if you subject your skin to a coating of concealing makeup day after day.

THE QUESTION OF DIET

Here is one of the hardest of all problems for the victim of acne to deal with. It is a time-honored tradition that certain foods will invariably wreak havoc on your complexion and if eaten at all will immediately bring forth a florid blossoming of acne. The forbidden foods? Chocolate in any form. Nuts or peanut butter. Any fried or greasy foods, such as hamburgers, french fries, or potato chips. Cheese foods, such as pizza. Milk or milk products, such as ice cream. In fact, virtually *all the foods that young people especially love to eat.*

What does modern medicine have to say of these diabolical dietary restrictions? Until very recently, doctors themselves were among the first to perpetuate the "bad food" theory of acne, subjecting their unhappy patients to rigid diets as a vital part of their treatment program. But recently more and more acne specialists have been disputing the notion that certain foods aggravate acne. A wide variety of scientific studies has shown little or no correlation between the severity of acne and the eating of the so-called bad foods. Some experts even contend that the whole idea of "forbidden foods" is nothing more than an unconscious method of punishing young people for their "wickedness" in getting acne and contend that no special food need be completely eliminated from the diet of acne sufferers. Writing in the medical journal *Post Graduate Medicine* in February 1974, Dr. Albert M. Kligman and his co-workers at the University of Pennsylvania stated their convictions bluntly:

> *No dietary item should be completely restricted. Acne is rarely influenced by diet. The foods most commonly prohibited reveal how punitively society views the acne "leper." These are almost exclusively items that teenagers love: chocolate, carbonated beverages, nuts, fried foods, candy, ice cream. No one rails against spinach and white bread. The dietary rule is moderation, not exclusion. We have never seen a patient in whom we could, at will, induce an exacerbation [i.e., a flare-up of acne] with a blacklisted food, even one which the patient claimed was harmful. This applies particularly to chocolate. To forbid favorite foods is to invite sin. . . .**

And yet, you say, you *know* that eating so much as a sliver of chocolate will, in the space of eighteen hours, bring forth a

---

* Albert M. Kligman et al., "Acne Vulgaris, A Treatable Disease," *Post Graduate Medicine,* 55:99–105 (1974).

flowering of acne papules on your face as surely as thunder follows lightning. And indeed it may do precisely that—to *you.* There are a few select individuals who *do* happen to have a temporary hypersensitivity or *idiosyncrasy* (to use the medical term) to chocolate, or to one or another of the forbidden foods. In addition, certain chemicals do appear to have a bad effect on acne *in certain people,* though no one yet knows why. These include the iodides in iodized salt, for example, or the bromides in such headache remedies as Bromo-Seltzer or Triple Bromides. Only you can determine whether you have such an idiosyncrasy or not. Rather than blindly (and perhaps unnecessarily) giving up any and all foods that you have heard might aggravate acne, try a simple experiment. Once your acne is under reasonable control with the simple home-treatment program we have outlined, try testing these forbidden foods *in moderation,* one by one, to see whether or not one or another has a significant effect on your complexion. Don't devour an entire sixteen-ounce chocolate bar at once as a test; take a bite or two, or a small glass of chocolate milk, as the "test dose." Do the same, one by one, with other foods. Then if you feel that one or another food does indeed aggravate your acne, perhaps you have found a food to which you, individually, are sensitive, and which you should avoid. But you may also find that you can safely eat and enjoy many supposedly forbidden foods, in moderation, at least occasionally.

Meanwhile, follow good rules of nutrition in your regular eating habits. Make sure that you have enough meat or other protein, cereals or breads, green leafy vegetables, and fruit or fruit juices every day. Take meals at regular intervals without skipping any. Avoid fake fad diets and keep away from the so-called empty snack foods (cakes and pastries, cheese puffs, tortilla chips, potato chips, and the like) that make no real contribution to your nutrition. A clear and healthy skin is rarely threatened by individual foods, but it does depend on adequate healthy nourishment. Malnourishment can be bad not only for your skin but for the rest of you as well.

THE PART
NERVES PLAY

Finally, a word should be said about another time-honored notion: that acne can be made worse, in some mysterious way, by nerves. Here we find a small kernel of truth in the midst of a lot of nonsense. Many girls do indeed find that their acne flares up a few days before the beginning of their menstrual periods, due to a natural shifting of the balance of hormones that is taking place at that time. This is also a time when many girls feel more tense and nervous than usual, more moody or emotionally changeable—again as a result of changing hormonal influences. It is easy to blame the acne on "nervousness" when in fact both the nervousness and the acne are caused by deep-seated hormonal adjustments.

In addition, there are boys and girls who complain that their acne tends to become worse during times of tension—the week before a big exam, for instance, or before an important athletic event or a major date. Thus the idea that nervousness can influence acne, to some extent, cannot be completely discarded. At worst, however, the influence is very limited and any increase in acne on this account will respond to basic simple home treatment.

There is, however, one way that nerves can have a more direct effect on acne. This is in the case of the "nervous picker," the individual who has developed a nervous habit of continually picking and playing with the skin of the face—poking, rubbing, touching, or scratching. This habit, like nail biting, hair twisting, or thumb sucking, can be very difficult to get rid of. The first step is to recognize that it can indeed be harmful (as well as unsightly) and can make even a mild case of acne worse. Then you must make a serious, conscious effort to *stop picking* every time you become aware of doing it. No medicine or any other device will be particularly helpful, but the realization that this habit can make a hated skin condition worse, or perpetuate it when it might be clearing up, should be sufficient to encourage the "nervous picker" to make the necessary effort to stop. You are hurting no one but yourself.

Medical Treatment

For many of you, the simple and basic home-treatment program will provide all the acne control that is necessary throughout the acne years. But what if you are one of the unlucky ones? Your acne, comparatively minor and controllable at first, has become suddenly and inexplicably worse. Whereas before you were bothered only with an occasional blemish, you are now developing a whole crop of red, raised papules. A great many of your pores seem to be blocked with blackheads and a number of whiteheads are appearing. Perhaps some of these seem larger and deeper than others, and some that are healing have taken on an unsightly purplish appearance and seem to be denting or drawing in the skin. Perhaps, in addition, you have a number of acne blemishes appearing on the nape of the neck, the chest, or the shoulders that do not seem to respond to conservative treatment at all. In short, the basic home-treatment program you have been using is no longer doing the job. The time has come to consult a doctor.

The first question, of course, is what kind of a doctor? Either an experienced family practitioner or a dermatologist (a specialist in skin diseases) would be a good choice. Most family practitioners today have had ample experience dealing with acne and have access to the latest and most up-to-date treatment methods available. Unfortunately, family practitioners also have a great many other kinds of illnesses competing for their attention and interest; many may not be as interested in dealing with acne as a dermatologist would be, and some may even consider it a nuisance. Since successful treatment in a difficult case depends greatly on the interest and perseverance of the doctor as well as the patient, you should try to pick a doctor, whether a family practitioner or a specialist, who seems genuinely interested in dealing with the problem and confident that it can be improved—as indeed it can.

Everything would be much simpler if there were one single medical approach to treatment that always worked no matter how severe the acne. Unfortunately, this is not the case. In fact, there are half a dozen different medical approaches to the treatment of acne. Each has its own special dangers or drawbacks, and hence can only be undertaken with a doctor's guidance. Each, on the other hand, has it own special advantages, and many doctors will use two or more medical approaches at the same time when dealing with stubborn cases.

Whichever medical approach or approaches your doctor may select, you should bear certain things in mind. First, any or all of these "big gun" treatments are usually prescribed *in addition to* the basic, conservative home-treatment program of skin cleansing and drying that you are already acquainted with. Medical treatment is simply aimed at accomplishing more in a faster amount of time in those cases where more needs to be accomplished. Second, the basic home-treatment program is essentially *symptomatic* treatment, dealing primarily with the unpleasant surface manifestations of acne. Medical treatment, on the other hand, seeks to go to the root of the problem—reduction in the size and activity of the sebaceous glands and/or reduction in the amount of infection present in those glands. Thus, although these approaches to treatment may be more costly and require occasional visits to a doctor, they can be expected to be effective in those difficult cases in which simple conservative home care just is not adequate.

ANTIBIOTIC THERAPY

Although the basic home-treatment program helps to keep the skin comparatively free of bacteria, dirt, oil, and debris, it does not attack the bacteria that are already growing in the sebaceous glands. This can be accomplished only by treatment with antibiotics.

What are the major bacterial offenders? Ordinary staphylococcus organisms are always present on the skin, even though it is thoroughly and regularly cleansed. Sometimes these organisms are involved in acne. More often, however, the offending organism is a bacillus known as *Corynebacterium acnes* that lives and thrives in the oil ducts and glands. Surface cleansing does little to hinder the growth of this organism, but internal antibiotics can. Today the antibiotic most commonly used for this purpose is *tetracycline,* one of the potent earth-mold antibiotics that strike at a wide range of different bacteria. Of all such antibiotics, tetracycline is the one that seems least likely to cause allergic reactions or other unfavorable effects in the body, and thus is the safest for long-term use. When it is prescribed for the treatment of acne, tetracycline is usually first ordered in a full treatment dose (one 250-milligram capsule four times a day) for a week or two—ample time for the doctor to determine if the drug is helping. Thereafter the dose is generally reduced in half (one capsule morning and evening) for a period of two or three weeks and then perhaps reduced to a quarter dose (one capsule a day) to be continued indefinitely. At such dosages it can safely be taken for months on end by most patients.

When this treatment is effective, there is a marked reduction in the number and size of the acne papules, pustules, and abscesses within a matter of two to three weeks. Those that appear subsequently are smaller, quicker to go away, and less likely to leave scars. Some doctors maintain their acne patients on low dosages of tetracycline for *years* with good control of the acne and without untoward effects from the drug. If you are taking such a medication, however, you should watch for any sign of skin rash or itching that might signal a drug reaction. In addition, your doctor may order occasional laboratory tests to be sure that the drug is doing no internal harm.

Of all the major medical approaches to treatment of acne, prolonged tetracycline therapy is perhaps the most effective with the fewest side effects, and thus is the most widely used today. Even so, it should only be used in those cases where it is really necessary—and only a doctor is qualified to make this judgment. Occasionally other antibiotic agents may be used in place of tetracycline. Any such antibiotic treatment is aimed at one of the major root causes of acne: infection developing in the plugged-up, overactive sebaceous glands and surrounding tissues. When such infection is effectively suppressed, the acne cannot help but improve.

HORMONE THERAPY

Another of the root causes of acne—indeed, the major underlying cause—is hormone activity that stimulates the enlargement and overactivity of the sebaceous glands in the first place. Today we know that the offending hormones are *androgens*— the hormones that are produced by the sex glands in the male, but also are produced in smaller quantities in the ovaries and adrenal glands of the female, as a part of normal growth and development. It is also known that the *estrogens,* or female sex hormones, tend to counteract or "cancel out" the activity of androgens in stimulating enlargement of the sebaceous glands. (This is the reason that many girls have comparatively milder and less widespread acne than boys do.) Thus another medical way to treat acne is to administer additional amounts of estrogens, especially to girls who are old enough to have completed their sexual development and established a regular pattern of menstrual periods. (The estrogens contained in the oral contraceptive pills have precisely the same anti-acne effect; many young women taking those pills note a sudden improvement in their complexions.)

Unfortunately, there are reasons that doctors are cautious about administering estrogens for the treatment of acne. These are extremely powerful hormones, and their long-term effects are not yet clearly understood. In some young women the administration of additional estrogens may bring about salt and water retention, ankle swelling, and even menstrual disturbances. Until more is known about these hormones, many doctors are reluctant to prescribe them for young women in treatment of a comparatively minor disorder that presents no serious medical threat.

The use of estrogens to treat acne in males can be even more troublesome. Effective as estrogen may be, certain of the hormonal side effects—most notably, a temporary enlargement of the breasts—are not eagerly welcomed by boys. This breast enlargement, know as *gynecomastia,* goes away as soon as the estrogen therapy is stopped, but it can cause great unhappiness in the patient as long as it persists.

Thus estrogen therapy is used cautiously in females and is applied only for brief intervals in males if it is applied at all. Because estrogen therapy *is* effective in reducing the size and activity of the sebaceous glands, it may be used today for a short interval in combination with antibiotic therapy in an effort to suppress an exceptionally severe case of acne as quickly as possible. In any case, its use must be very closely monitored by an experienced physician.

VITAMIN THERAPY

For many years it has been known that large doses of vitamin A, taken internally, seem to cause improvement in certain acne patients, although no one knows precisely why. Huge doses —between 50,000 and 100,000 International Units daily for a period of several days, gradually increased to as much as 400,000 International Units daily before the dosage is again tapered off—are needed to be effective. (By comparison, the amount of vitamin A present in an ordinary once-daily vitamin capsule will range between 500 and 1000 International Units.) Unfortunately, vitamin A is one of the vitamins that can have adverse effects on the body when too much is taken for too long. For this reason high doses of vitamin A should *never* be taken except on specific instructions from a doctor and under a doctor's observation.

Vitamin A has never been widely used as an internal medicine for the treatment of acne. But in recent years a derivative of vitamin A known as *vitamin A acid, retinoic acid,* or *tretinoin* has been used very effectively by some dermatologists as a surface application for the control of severe acne. Tretinoin is an exceedingly irritating substance. Applied to the skin twice a day, even in tiny amounts (5/100 of 1 percent in a lotion base), it can cause a marked flushing and burning sensation, followed by drying and peeling. This substance gets rid of loose epithelial cells on the surface of the skin, hardens or toughens the underlying skin, successfully unseats existing comedones, and makes it difficult for new ones to form. As the skin becomes "seasoned" to this irritating agent, higher concentrations may safely be used at more frequent intervals. This is one instance in which the medication is used *in place* of any other drying agent or skin application; only the gentlest washing of the skin twice a day is allowed while it is being used. Tretinoin must be applied when the skin is dry so that not too much will be absorbed into the water-softened skin layers. In addition, it must be used together with a sun-screen lotion to protect against excessive sunburn.

When tretinoin therapy is used, improvement usually becomes evident after two to three weeks. Treatment is continued as long as the improvement continues. If the acne is exceptionally severe, the tretinoin therapy may be combined with antibiotic therapy, oral vitamin A therapy, or both. Until recently this new approach to acne treatment has been used largely by skin specialists, but today more and more family practitioners are becoming experienced in its use.

For all the promising results that tretinoin treatment seems to bring about, it is by no means the cure-all for acne. It is admittedly uncomfortable and unpleasant stuff to use, and there is not yet enough data to thoroughly assess its overall effectiveness. Certainly it is not for every acne sufferer, but there is real hope that it may ultimately prove to be an enormous aid in the control of severe or intractable acne.

LIGHT AND RADIATION THERAPY

While such new approaches as tretinoin therapy come into vogue, certain other "time-honored" forms of medical treatment have fallen into disrepute today and are mentioned here mainly for their historic interest. Among these are *ultraviolet light therapy* and *X-ray therapy*.

The idea of treating acne with ultraviolet light arose from the widespread observation that acne in many individuals

seemed to improve markedly during the summer months, following regular exposure to the sun, and to become worse again during the gray winter months. Doctors reasoned that the ultraviolet radiation in the sunlight penetrated to the sebaceous glands and cut down their enlargement and activity. And, indeed, experiments proved that ultraviolet light treatment often did help cases of acne, but many problems were involved. Ordinarily, sunlamps of the home-treatment kind delivered far too little ultraviolet to do any good. Extremely powerful ultraviolet lamps were necessary, and since such lamps could deliver dangerous burns in a matter of a few *minutes* of overexposure, such treatment could only be provided in a doctor's office. Because treatment was required every other day for prolonged periods, the cost could become prohibitive. What was more, the beneficial effects disappeared as soon as the therapy was stopped. Thus today ultraviolet light therapy is rarely used except occasionally as an adjunct to other forms of therapy, in hope of achieving results more quickly.

X-ray therapy had even more drawbacks. There was no question that deep-penetrating X-rays were capable of counteracting the enlargement and excessive oil secretion of sebaceous glands effectively and permanently, and there was a time twenty or thirty years ago when a great many acne patients received this kind of treament. Gradually, however, doctors came to realize that such X-ray treatment could do more harm than good. Intense exposure to X-rays could, for example, lead to cancer of the skin, the thyroid, or the bone marrow. Today X-ray specialists believe that the use of X-rays should be reserved exclusively for necessary diagnostic studies, or for the intensive treatment of certain kinds of cancers, and should never be used for less life-threatening conditions such as acne. In fact, some specialists have recently been urging that people who received X-ray therapy for acne years ago should see a physician for special screening tests for their own protection against possible cancer.

CORTISONE TREATMENT

There was a time soon after the discovery of the cortisone hormones in the 1940s when cortisone was widely tested in the treatment of acne. It was thought that cortisone, which tended to suppress many kinds of inflammatory reactions in the body, might suppress the inflammation associated with acne as well. Exactly the opposite was found, however. Cortisone taken internally actually proved to make acne worse, and its use as a surface-acting cream provided no benefit. Today dermatologists will occasionally inject a tiny amount of hydrocortisone directly *into* a large cystic acne lesion to help speed its healing. Otherwise, the cortisone drugs are not considered an aid to acne treatment.

SURGICAL TREATMENT

Occasionally it proves necessary to open and drain large cysts or abscesses caused by acne. Obviously this sort of surgical treatment must depend upon a doctor's judgment and—thanks to other remedies that prevent such lesions from arising—it is becoming less and less necessary.

Another kind of surgical treatment, however, can sometimes be useful to help repair severe scarring of the face or other skin surfaces. This procedure is known as *dermabrasion* (literally, "skin scraping"). With the patient under anesthesia, the surgeon uses abrasive substances to "sand down" scars and bumps in the diseased skin, thus inducing normal, healthy skin to grow back in its place. In some cases the end results are excellent. In others they are not so excellent. Sometimes the new skin is different in pigmentation from the surrounding skin, causing unsightly blotches. Sometimes new scarring occurs in place of the old. If you are one who has suffered severe scarring and disfigurement on account of acne, you should certainly discuss this approach to treatment with a dermatologist, preferably in consultation with a plastic surgeon. But you should fully understand the possible ill effects before undertaking any such treatment. Most often the wiser course is to wait and give nature a chance. Undertake vigorous treatment of any residual acne in order to prevent additional scarring and disfigurement, and allow sufficient time for the old scars to shrink. If a procedure such as dermabrasion is really indicated, it will still be indicated five years later and will be just as effective then, if not more so, than if it were undertaken prematurely now.

Clear Skin and Good Grooming

Few young people today think it necessary to be beautiful or strikingly handsome. For most, it is enough to have a comfortable self-image and to be confident that they are making the best of the attractive qualities that they do possess.

The control of acne and the achievement of a clear and healthy skin goes a long way toward meeting the personal appearance goals of most young people. But acne is not the only troublesome grooming problem. The maintenance of a clear, healthy skin depends upon more than just control of acne, and other disturbances ranging all the way from dandruff to body odor must be dealt with. Fortunately, with a little effort and application most of these problems are easily solved.

VITAMINS, NUTRITION, AND HEALTHY SKIN

As we have seen, the experts today believe that acne is affected very little, if at all, by the specific foods that you eat. But quite aside from acne, what you choose to eat, and how, *can* have considerable effect on the overall appearance of your skin, to say nothing of the overall health of your body. Yet young people are notoriously negligent of the most simple principles of good nutrition. They tend to gorge themselves when they are hungry and to turn up their noses at nutritious meals when they're not. They tend to snack incessantly, and a great many seem to subsist almost solely upon hamburgers and french fries, pizzas, milk, and carbonated beverages. As a result a great many youngsters put on weight that they do not need, ruin their teeth, and malnourish their bodies—and then wonder why they have skin problems.

Good nutrition is not all that difficult to achieve. Here are some basic, common-sense rules to follow:

1. Eat *some* kind of breakfast before you charge off to the day's activities. Nobody needs bacon and eggs every day, but you *do* need some type of cereal, fruit, and milk for breakfast. Don't stuff yourself, but don't skip, either.

2. Eat *something* for lunch besides vending-machine snacks.

3. When you snack after school (less urgently necessary if you have eaten an adequate lunch) try to confine yourself to a sandwich, a salad, or a fruit instead of candy, cookies, cake, ice cream, or other comparatively empty (that is, nonnutritious) snacks.

4. Eat at least one fully balanced hot meal each day. Such a meal should include protein (meat or cheese), a vegetable, a carbohydrate (bread, potato, or rice), and, ideally, a fruit. If you are so hungry by dinner time that you must stuff yourself, this can only mean that you're cheating your diet (and starving yourself) the rest of the day. Eat more every other meal in order to diminish the volume of food necessary at dinner time.

5. Take a daily vitamin supplement. A dozen brands of one-capsule-a-day vitamins are available at the supermarket or

drugstore; consult your doctor, your pharmacist, or your school nurse regarding precise brands and preparations. Don't waste your money on so-called therapeutic or extra-high-potency vitamins or vitamin-and-mineral preparations unless your doctor specifically prescribes them.

6. Weigh yourself once a week, if you are slender, to see that your weight is not getting out of control and *once a day* if you are even slightly overweight. Obesity can be as unattractive and heartbreaking as acne, and a great deal worse for your general health. Excess weight during the teen years can easily be controlled by spacing meals more evenly throughout the day and by increasing protein foods and vegetables, reducing the total intake of carbohydrates and fats, and cutting down sharply on the snack foods, such as corn chips, sugar candies, sugar frosted cereals, french fries, and so forth. These foods are fine once in a while for a treat; as a steady diet, five times a day, they simply don't make sense.

If excess weight is a problem that doesn't seem to yield to the kind of simple control outlined above, you should consult a doctor, follow his or her recommendations, and enlist your parents' support in a sensible, continuing diet program. Avoid crash diets and fad diets like the plague; they will not *keep* your weight down, and they can very easily make you sick.

THE PROBLEM OF DANDRUFF

If acne is a common grooming problem among young people, *seborrheic dermatitis* or common dandruff is perhaps even more widespread. Once again it is the sebaceous oil-forming glands that are at fault, this time in the scalp where they are far more numerous than anywhere else. The sebum, ever-present on the scalp, can cake and crust the epidermal cells that are naturally peeling off. This mixture of oil and dead organic matter is a splendid medium for the growth of a variety of surface bacteria to be found on the scalp. The result is a scaly, slightly itchy surface inflammation of the scalp. In mild cases it may appear as nothing more than an annoying "snowfall" of white dandruff scale; in more severe cases there may be widespread crusted areas on the scalp and occasionally deeper-seated infection as well. The dermatitis tends to follow the hairline and frequently involves the eyebrows, the eyelashes, the sideburns, or the beard as well as the scalp.

What can you do about dandruff? From the multitudes of so-called dandruff remover shampoos, hairdressings, and scalp treatments that you will find crowding the shelves of your local drugstore, you can be pretty certain that there is no single universally successful treatment. Even dermatologists concede that dandruff may not be curable. It is, however, controllable.

The approach you should follow depends upon the severity of the problem:

1. In minor cases—perhaps 70 percent of all cases—good control can be achieved by use of a good nonmedicated detergent shampoo twice or three times a week. Most of the shampoos available in the drugstore or supermarket work well in either hard or soft water, but extra care should be taken rinsing hair in hard water areas to be sure that soap curds do not remain trapped. Just dousing the hair in the school shower after a physical education class is not enough; it is the *scalp* you want to cleanse with thorough scrubbing. If you feel that one of the so-called protein shampoos leaves your hair more manageable after shampooing, by all means use it—but see that the scalp is well scrubbed just the same.

This procedure will clear away loose dandruff, rinse away

excess oils from the hair, and provide bacteria with a poorer environment for growth. After shampooing and drying your hair thoroughly, use a comb for the initial grooming. If any evidence of dandruff residue appears on the comb during this process, you obviously haven't cleared away all the debris and you'd better repeat the shampoo. Avoid oily, greasy, or sticky hair-grooming preparations after your shampoo. After all, you have just gone to considerable effort to get *rid* of all the guck in your hair, so don't deliberately plaster it down with more. Most people can use plain water for grooming the hair after a shampoo. For those with exceedingly fine hair that tends to stand out in all directions when dry, a *small* amount of one of the so-called dry-grooming preparations may be used—but keep the amount small. All of these preparations leave a certain residue on the hair and scalp and may, in some cases, even contribute to the dandruff.

2. If simple shampooing doesn't provide control of dandruff, try one or more of the medicated dandruff remover shampoos that are available over the counter in the drugstore. Certain of these preparations contain small amounts of *selenium,* a potent antidandruff medication. Selenium is a poison when taken internally and can also cause surface irritation of the scalp in certain people. Such a selenium-containing shampoo should be used only once a week, with an ordinary shampoo used the other times, and great care should be taken to rinse the hair thoroughly after shampooing. Any such medicated preparation should be discontinued at once if there is any sign of persistent soreness, burning, or irritation of the scalp after shampooing.

3. In problem cases with actively crusting dermatitis of the scalp, scalp irritation, weeping of the scalp surface, or persistent and exceptionally heavy dandruff, consult a doctor. He may find it necessary to prescribe surface medications to be rubbed into the scalp to help reduce the amount, severity, or degree of infection of the dermatitis. He may also prescribe an extra-strength selenium-containing shampoo, with instructions for leaving the preparation in contact with the scalp for an interval of time while shampooing before rinsing it out.

No single method will always knock dandruff out completely. With a little care and attention, however, it can generally be kept under control indefinitely.

CONTROLLING
BODY ODOR

The adolescent years are not only the time when acne appears, but are also the time when underarm odor can become a problem. The same hormonal changes that bring about acne also bring about an enlargement and overactivity of sweat glands in such areas as the groin, behind the ears, or under the arms. Underarm odor in particular tends to be offensive during these years, but can almost always be controlled with a little care and attention. Attention to cleanliness is the first rule. The underarms should be washed with soap and water twice a day whether you are bathing at the same time or not. There is no objective evidence that specially medicated antibacterial or deodorant soaps are any more effective, in the long run, than ordinary inexpensive facial soap, but if they make you feel more confident there is no reason not to use them. Then, after drying the underarms, a cream or spray deodorant can be applied. Any one of dozens of such preparations are available; use whichever one you find to be most effective. Bear in mind, however, that the antiperspirant and deodorant chemicals in these preparations can, in some cases, cause troublesome skin irritation. Girls who have just shaved their armpits should wait perhaps twelve hours before applying a deodorant, and anyone who observes persisting redness, soreness, or itching following the use of a deodorant preparation should discontinue it and seek a nonirritating substitute. In addition, you must weigh the effectiveness of the deodorant against the cost of replacing stained or damaged clothing. Despite advertising claims, virtually all of the antiperspirant and deodorant preparations will cause a certain amount of staining and damage to the clothing. This can be minimized, of course, by using the minimum amount of deodorant necessary at any given time.

SUNTAN AND
HEALTHY SKIN

America is a nation of summer sun worshipers, and teen-agers are perhaps more avid in their search for an attractive summer tan than anyone else. Among other things, thorough and regular sun drenching during the summer months helps keep acne under control—but as with so many other things, the cosmetic and therapeutic benefits of suntanning are accompanied by some less-than-desirable side effects.

Nothing need be said here about the special agonies of sunburn; if you have not already learned for yourself what sunburn can do, all you will need is one good, murderous exposure to teach you respect for the sun for the rest of your life.

The alternative to sunburn, of course, is tanning, which is achieved by frequent repeated exposures to the sun, first for short intervals, then for lengthening periods of time. Unfortunately, however, dermatologists are virtually unanimous in condemning suntanning as basically harmful to the skin and complexion. And indeed, there is considerable evidence that a deep summer tan is something that people who are concerned with the health of their skin should find a way to do without.

The reasons are simple. Tanning is a response of the pigment cells in the skin to the ultraviolet radiation from the sun. But this radiation affects more than just the pigment cells: it can also cause change and damage to the elastic and collagen fibers in the skin, the tissue that keeps the skin soft, supple, and elastic. With repeated tanning, the skin becomes progressively thicker, more dense, tougher, drier, and less elastic. Since these changes are, to a certain degree, irreversible, the minor damage that occurs during one summer will be compounded by additional minor damage the next summer, and the next, and so on.

The long-term result can be skin damage of a major degree. It has been estimated that deep tanning during one summer ages the skin five years. Repeated tanning leads to premature wrinkling, coarsening, and toughening of the skin, and the complexion suffers accordingly. In addition, excessive ultraviolet radiation can cause changes in the skin cells that can lead to the development of skin cancers over a period of years.

The solution, obviously, is moderation. A deep tan, however cosmetically desirable, is dangerous to the health of your skin. Moderate your skin exposure; when you are exposed, protect your skin from radiation with one of the so-called sunscreen lotions your pharmacist can recommend; and be willing to settle for a rosy summer glow rather than a black-brown tan. The skin you save may be your own.

For Further Reading

Bobroff, Arthur, M.D. *Acne: And Related Disorders of Complexion and Scalp.* Springfield, Ill.: Charles C. Thomas, 1964.

Nourse, Alan E., M.D. *Ladies' Home Journal Family Medical Guide.* New York: Harper & Row, 1973. Chapter 31.

Sauer, Gordon C., M.D. *Teen Skin.* Springfield, Ill.: Charles C. Thomas, 1965.

Sternberg, Thomas H., M.D. *More Than Skin Deep.* New York: Doubleday, 1970.

Sutton, Richard L., Jr., M.D. *The Skin: A Handbook.* New York: Doubleday, 1962.

Index

Dermatitis, 24
Dermatologists, 36
Dermis, 12–13
Diet, 5, 28–31, 48–50
Dieting, 49–50
    crash, 50
Drying agents, 25

Elastic tissue, 13, 54
Epidermis, 10
Estrogen therapy, 39
Estrogens, 14, 38–39

Foods, 5, 28–31, 48–50

Gynecomastia, 39

Hair care, 26–27
Hair follicle, 12
Hormone activity, 14, 18–19, 21
Hormone therapy, 38–40
Hydrocortisone, 44
Hygiene, 4
Hypersensitivity, 31

Kligman, Albert M., 30

Makeup, 18, 27–28
Medical treatment, 35–45
Melanin, 12
Menstruation, 19, 32

Nerve endings, 10
Nerves, 32–33

Nutrition, 31, 48–50

Oral contraceptive pills, effect on complexion of, 39

Papules, 16, 22, 26
Perspiration, 10, 13
Phenol, 25
pHisoHex, 24
Pigment cells, 12, 54–55
Pores, 15, 22
Prescription medications, 19
Puberty, 14
Pustules, 16, 22, 26

Reducing weight, 49–50
Retinoic acid, 40

Scalp care, 26–27
Scarring, 1, 4, 19, 44
Sebaceous glands, 10, 12, 15, 18, 21–22
Seborrheic dermatitis, 50
Sebum, 10, 12, 15, 18, 21–22
Selenium, 52
Septisol, 24
Sex hormones, 14, 18–19, 21
Sexual maturation, and acne, 4–5, 14–15
Shampoos, 50–53
Skin
    function of, 9–10
    structures of, 10–14
    tanning, 54–55
Skin cancer, 55

About the Author

Alan Nourse, well-known author of books for young people, turned to writing after his career as a practicing physician. His other books for Franklin Watts on medical topics include *Lumps, Bumps, and Rashes: A Look at Kids' Diseases* (A First Book) and *Viruses* (A First Book). Dr. Nourse is also noted for his science fiction and books on astronomy.

The author lives with his wife and four children in the state of Washington, where he enjoys his hobbies of fishing and backpacking.